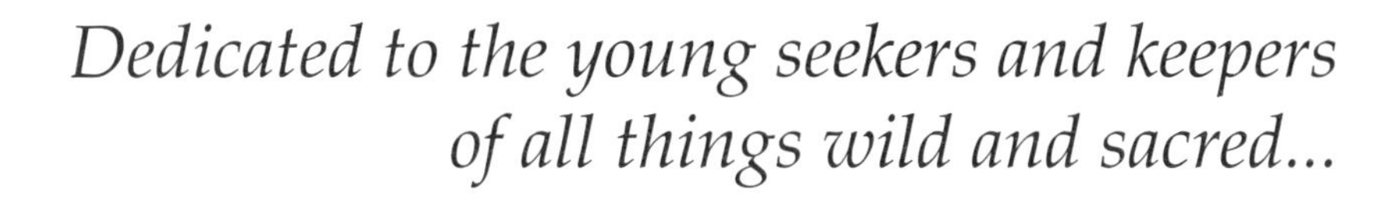

by Biff Baird & Judy Rosen

Biff Baird earns his living as an interpretive planner, freelance writer, and exhibit designer. A father of two, he prefers hiking, mountain-biking, skiing, and scuba-diving to working. Judy Rosen began her National Park Service career at Canyon de Chelly National Monument. She has worked as a naturalist and planner in many national parks and forests. She raises two sons while working at Rocky Mountain National Park.

Illustrations by Loren Purcell

Loren Purcell, a second-generation wildlife artist, has been drawing for 20 years. From the time he picked up a crayon at age 6, he has found his voice through art. Now working full-time as an artist and serving as illustrator for the 19th Special Forces, he and his wife jointly operate their own studio in Henderson, Nevada.

Front cover: A ranger-led hike is a great way to learn about the park.
Inside front cover: An arch of stone is a door into another world. Title page: Mountain chickadee.

Edited by Cheri C. Madison. Book design by Stuart Martin.
Series design by K. C. DenDooven.

LC 20-010863. ISBN 0-88714-218-4.

From the shadows of the canyons
To rocks that greet the sun,
Winds blow and do not sleep—
Nature's work is never done.

All About Bryce Canyon

Bryce Canyon National Park is set on the brink of a fairyland. Rocks spring up before your eyes in amazing shapes. *Hoodoos*, like soldiers of stone in a row, salute you.

It took 65 million years for wind and water to sculpt this canyon into cathedrals, temples, spires, and arches. Their colors change moment to moment, and shadows cast eerie magic on mazes and slot canyons below. It's time to explore!

What lies around the next bend of Peekaboo Trail? How about a walk down the pink cliffs of the *Grand Staircase*? Does Silent City remind you of ruins of an ancient civilization?

Let your mind travel to far corners of the world as you view formations like the Chinese Wall and Queen's Garden. Bryce Canyon is a place where you can see forever . . . It is a fairyland of rocks . . . and so much more.

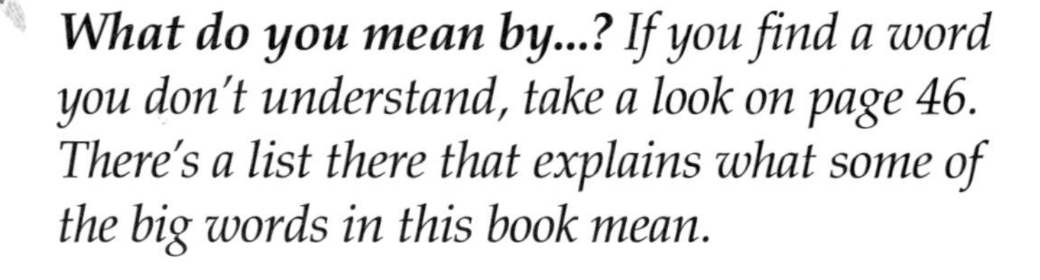

What do you mean by...? *If you find a word you don't understand, take a look on page 46. There's a list there that explains what some of the big words in this book mean.*

A is for the **Amphitheater**—
Hoodoos standing in their rows
Like people made of colored rocks
At concerts and puppet shows.

Bryce Brims with History

Bryce Canyon echoes the lives of people who passed this way long before us. Over 12,000 years ago, hunters tracked woolly mammoth and camels that once roamed this area.

Others would follow as the centuries passed. *Desert Archaic*, *Basket Maker*, and *Pueblo peoples*, *Paiutes*, and pioneers found game, nuts, berries, and timber plentiful here. How do you think they felt when they caught their first glimpse of Bryce Canyon?

The Paiute Indians called these badlands *Unka-timpe-wa-wince-pock-ich*—"red rocks standing like men in a bowl-shaped recess." According to a Paiute story, *hoodoos* are people turned to stone by angry gods.

Beautiful as it is, few people made permanent homes here. It's too high, rugged, and cold. Like winds that whistle through the rocks, most people just passed through.

Watch your step! There are many steep drop-offs in Bryce.

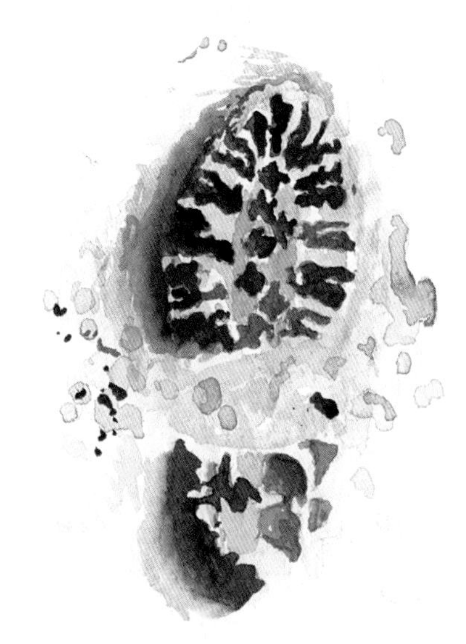

B is for **Bryce Canyon**
Of towering red-cliffed heights.
Canyons, castles, cathedrals, and cliffs...
Sunlit days and starry nights.

C is for the **Chinese Wall**.
Water and wind shaped its heights
Over more time than we can imagine—
Millions of days, millions of nights.

D is for the **Deer**.
They watch, listen, sniff the air—
Always ready to take flight
If they sense that danger's there.

Extraordinary Evidence of Erosion

Let's pretend that you've got a huge cake pan, and your parents don't care if you make a mess. OK?

Cover the bottom of the pan with sand. Throw in some seashells and pour river mud over everything. Then put in a layer of rocks and gravel. Cover it all with some of the gooey muck from the bottom of a lake. Let it sit until it gets really hard—a few million years. It'll crack a little.

Now imagine that you're super-strong. Push on the pan from both ends until it bends up in the middle to make a hill, just like the crust of the earth sometimes gets pushed up.

Get a watering can and sprinkle water over the top for awhile. See how it runs down the cracks and makes gullies in the side of the hill? And exposes the different layers of stuff so you can see them? That's *erosion*.

And that's one reason why Bryce Canyon looks the way it does.

E is for **Erosion**.
Even mountains wear away.
Water carries off a bit
Of Bryce Canyon every day.

F is for **Fairyland**
Where you can see the hoodoos.
If they are people turned to stone,
Are there medoos, theydoos, or youdoos?

F

G is for the **Ground Squirrels**.
Look for them in forest places.
Some people think they're chipmunks,
But they have no stripes upon their faces.

G

How Hoodoos Happen

Remember pouring water over the hill you made in the cake pan?

You probably noticed that some stuff got washed away faster than other stuff. That's called *differential erosion*, and that's what makes *hoodoos*.

Put a flat piece of concrete on top of your hill. Sprinkle water over everything again. Do you see how the stuff right underneath the concrete doesn't get washed away? Keep pouring, and you'll wind up with a tower of softer stuff underneath the concrete. You made a hoodoo! The piece on top is called a *cap rock*.

If you took the pan and froze it, your wet hoodoo might crack. That's what happens in Bryce Canyon when melting snow seeps into cracks on a winter day. The water freezes at night, expands, and the cracks get bigger. That's called frost-wedging.

And that's another reason why Bryce Canyon looks the way it does.

H is for the **Hoodoos**.
Try to read them like a book.
Wind, frost, and water carved them.
Can you guess how long it took?

H

Ignite Your Imagination!

Wild places call to us. They take us away from our daily routine. They make us feel happy. They make us feel humble. And they also spark our imagination. With a fairyland of rocks before you, there is no place like Bryce Canyon to imagine!

Thor's Hammer. The Alligator. Silent City. The Poodle. People put names to such amazing formations to make them feel familiar to us, to bring their grandeur to a size we can absorb.

Gaze out over the horizon, and make up your own names for the countless rocks before you. Better yet, explore them up close. Your own stories might unfold . . . just like a fairyland.

On the edge of Inspiration Point, what does Bryce Canyon stir inside of you?

This great world of rocks looks different from the top than it does from the bottom. Your own names for the same rock may change, depending on your vantage point.

I is for **Inspiration Point**,
Where you can stop and gaze.
What's it like way down below
Hiking through a red-rock maze?

I

Just for Kids!

Become a Junior Ranger. It's easy and fun. Join a ranger for games and activities about Bryce Canyon. All you need to do is sign up at the Visitor Center, pick up a workbook and do the activities, collect a bag of litter, and attend a ranger-led program.

Then return to the Visitor Center for your special Junior Ranger badge, patch, and certificate.

Junior Rangers:

* help keep national parks clean.
* learn all they can about the park.
* show respect for nature.

YOU can become the next Junior Ranger at Bryce Canyon National Park!

What do you mean by...? *If you find a word you don't understand, take a look on page 46. There's a list there that explains what some of the big words in this book mean.*

J is for **Junior Ranger**.
It's easy to become one.
Play games, explore, and learn new stuff,
Protect the park, and have some fun.

K is for the **Kestrel**,
A small bird of prey
That hovers on rapidly-beating wings
The colors of blue and gray.

K

L is for the **Lightning**.
It's beautiful, but scary too!
If it's crackling, run inside—
That's the safest thing to do.

L

Making the Desert Bloom

The *Mormon* pioneers who settled Bryce Valley didn't have an easy time of it. They had to travel over a week by wagon for basic supplies like salt, nails, or sugar. In winter, they were totally cut off from the rest of the world.

But they made the desert bloom. With picks, shovels, and horse-drawn scrapers they built dams and miles of ditches to bring precious water to fields and gardens. They grew corn, wheat, and vegetables. They planted orchards. They built roads to the high *plateaus* and cut timber to build homes. They survived.

Ebenezer and Mary Ann Bryce—early settlers for whom this canyon was named—called these badlands "a hell of a place to lose a cow!"

But the pioneers' success meant disaster for the *Paiute*, who depended on the seeds of Indian ricegrass for food. The pioneers' sheep and cattle ate most of the ricegrass. Only a few years after the first log cabin was built in Bryce Valley, the Paiute were forced to move on from a land they had called home for centuries.

M is for the **Mormon settlers**,
Who pioneered this dry, dry land.
They farmed their fields and grazed their cows
And lived in cabins built by hand.

M

There are deep caverns and rooms . . .
spires, and steeples . . .
presenting the wildest and most wonderful
scene that the eye of man ever beheld, in
fact it is one of the wonders of the world.
-T. C. Bailey, 1877

N is for **Natural Bridge**.
How many ticks of a clock
Did snow and rainstorms take to make
This giant hole in the rock?

N

O is for the **Owls**,
Hooting in the night.
Come explore while they're awake
Under stars that twinkle bright.

Pine-Topped Plateaus

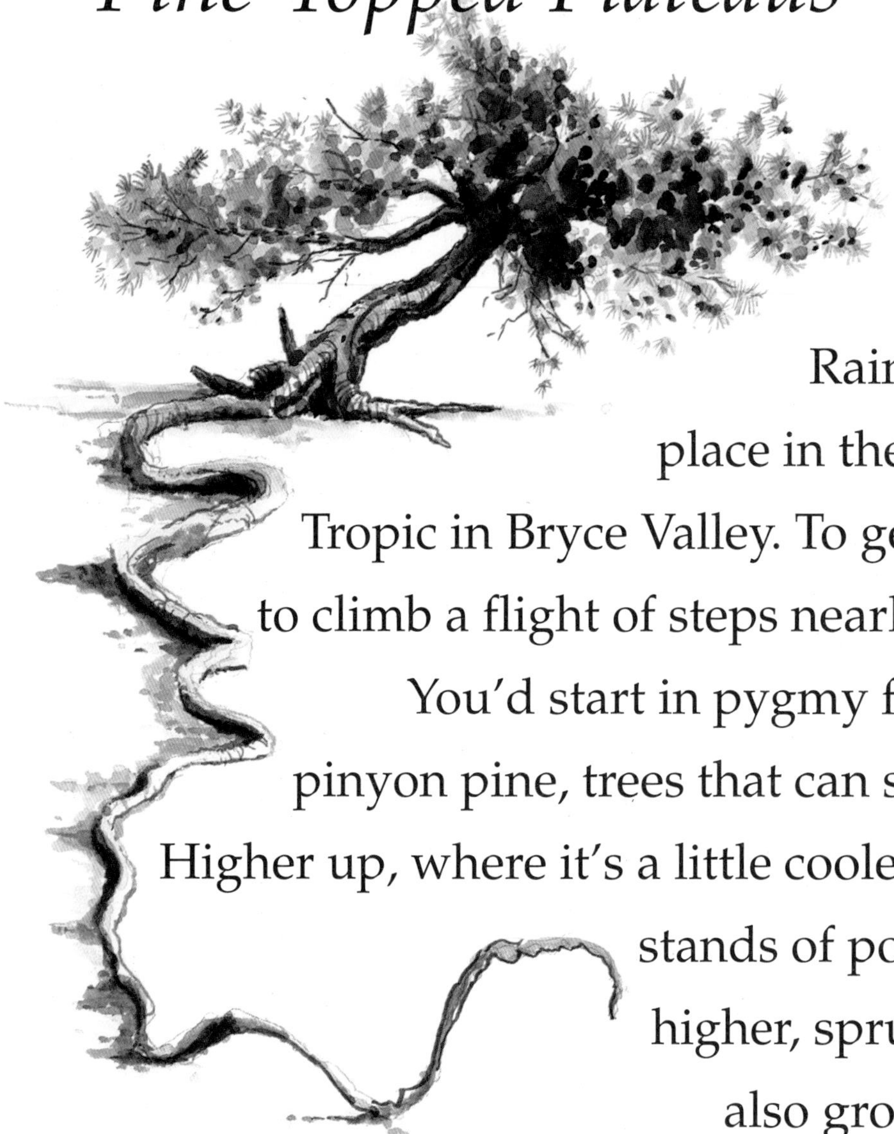

Suppose there was a great big slide that dropped from Rainbow Point (the highest place in the park) to the town of Tropic in Bryce Valley. To get to the top, you'd have to climb a flight of steps nearly 3,000 feet high!

You'd start in pygmy forests of juniper and pinyon pine, trees that can survive heat and drought. Higher up, where it's a little cooler and wetter, are stands of ponderosa pine. Even higher, spruce and fir trees (that also grow way up north in Canada) can be found.

Branches of the limber pine are very flexible so they can bend in strong winds without breaking.

Bristlecone and limber pines live at the top of the slide. Their twisted branches speak of bitter cold and harsh winds. Some of the park's gnarly bristlecones are more than a thousand years old!

The trees in each kind of evergreen forest you climbed through are adapted to a different climate and type of soil. That was a long, steep climb. Ready to slide down?

P is for the **Ponderosa Pine**.
Why don't you give its bark a sniff?
Yummy vanilla fills your nose
If you take a whiff.

P

Queens, Castles, and Critters

How about a hike to the Queen's Garden? A stroll to the Sentinel? Or a snooze in the sun with the Alligator?

Each of these formations shows the process of *differential erosion*. Softer layers wear away more quickly than harder ones, making the shapes that spark our imaginations.

The Sentinel

The Queen looks over her garden, but will she outlive it? How long will the Alligator's nap last? If we come back to see the Sentinel in 50 years, will it still be on guard, or will it be just another mound of dirt?

Bryce Canyon is a storybook with a surprise waiting whenever time turns a page. What will your children and grandchildren discover when they come to read this magical book of nature?

The Alligator

Q is for the **Queen's Garden**.
Imagine sitting on her throne
Gazing down at her majestic
Castles made of stone.

Q

Rabbits to Rabbitbrush

Greenleaf manzanita

What's that you just saw dash beneath the rabbitbrush? It could have been a chipmunk, squirrel, prairie dog, lizard, mouse, or gopher. Day and night, Bryce Canyon teems with critters. And critters depend on plants to survive.

Over 70 different plants provide food and shelter for wildlife at Bryce Canyon. The nuts and berries of pinyon and juniper trees feed jays, ground squirrels, deer mice, and wood rats. These animals, in turn, are eaten by ring-tailed cats, foxes, and bobcats.

Manzanita shrubs shelter cottontails from coyotes, eagles, and mountain lions. They also are a favorite food for mule deer.

Wild iris, Indian paintbrush, rabbitbrush, groundsel, and cinquefoil not only add color to Bryce Canyon, but also mean life for the many birds and animals that live there.

If there weren't so many plants, would we see all these animals?

Reveal paintbrush

R is for the **Rabbitbrush**—
Yellow flowers greet the sun.
Watch quietly and carefully—
You might see a chipmunk run!

R

Sunrise to Sunset

Ready? Set? Sunrise! Let's get out there and have a look! From dawn till dusk, Bryce Canyon is a kaleidoscope of ever-changing color.

Why do you think this formation is known as Sinking Ship?

Sunrise and Sunset Points are great places to watch and take pictures of rock and sky. Early morning and late afternoon light enrich the natural colors and deepen the shadows in the fairyland of rock below.

Throughout the seasons, colors change the face of Bryce. In spring, flowers bloom at your feet in yellows, pinks, and whites. In summer, grasses green up the meadows against a deep blue sky. In autumn, the rocks burn golden, and red maple stands out against the aspen leaves. In winter, add bright white to blue sky, red rock, and deep green pines.

From sunrise to sunset, from spring to fall, Bryce Canyon bursts with color. Sunrise and Sunset Points are favorite places to witness it.

S is for **Sunrise Point**—
Catch the early morning glow.
Fiery colors streak the sky
And light the canyons down below.

S

T is for **Tower Bridge**,
Between two pillars standing tall.
Take a look while you're here...
Someday it's bound to fall!

T

U is for **Utah Prairie Dog**,
A species that's in danger.
To find out more about them,
You could ask a ranger.

U

Visitor Center Questions and Answers

Q: What makes the rocks the color pink?

A: Rust. Tiny particles of iron in the rock oxidize (rust) when they're exposed to the air, creating all kinds of different shades of pink and red.

Q: Is Bryce Canyon really a canyon?

A: No! The early settlers mistakenly called these fantastic badlands a canyon, and the name stuck. What people call Bryce Canyon is actually the eroded edge of the Paunsaugunt Plateau.

Q: If we've only got a few hours to see the park, what should we do?

A: Stop in at the visitor center to see the exhibits, watch a short video, and get a map. Then you could take a short drive to Sunrise, Sunset, Inspiration, and Bryce viewpoints. There are many areas to enjoy a picnic.

Q: What's a good short hike for kids?

A: Try walking the Rim Trail between Sunrise Point and Sunset Point. It's fairly level and has great views. If you want to go below the rim, Queen's Garden Trail from Sunrise Point is the easiest.

V is for the **Visitor Center**
Where you can go to ask:
What's that plant? Where should I hike?
Answers are the ranger's task.

Winter Wonderland

Perhaps the "coolest" season of all in Bryce is winter. Few people ever see it. Snow covers the piney plateau and caps the red rocks, outlining their fanciful shapes.

The road and overlooks are open. Hiking trails become havens for skiers and snowshoers.

Look for the nuthatch, a year-round resident. Watch deer descend into the valley below. Read the drama of life and death in the tracks of a mountain lion chasing a deer.

Visibility is best in winter. From the rim of Bryce, you can see up to 200 miles, even into Arizona and New Mexico.

All the colors of Bryce—green trees, red rocks, and blue sky—seem more brilliant in winter against a dazzling white blanket of snow. Picture yourself in this winter wonderland!

W is for **Winter**,
A wonderful time to see
Pines and hoodoos topped with snow.
Explore by snowshoe or by ski.

W

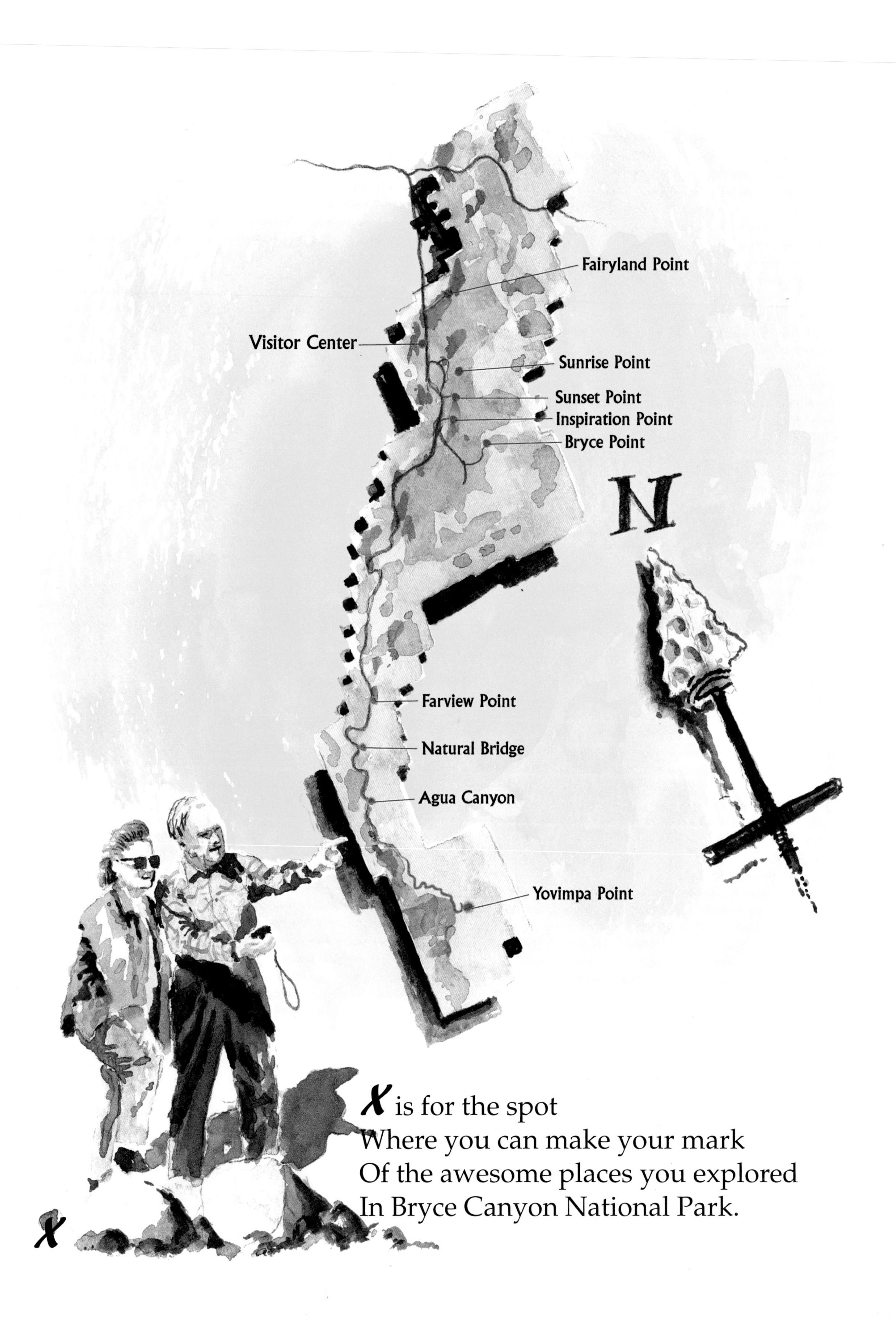

X is for the spot
Where you can make your mark
Of the awesome places you explored
In Bryce Canyon National Park.

Y is for **Yovimpa Point**
At the top of the Grand Staircase
That you could walk down if you were
A giant with a giant's pace.

Zillions of things we missed

There's way more things to do and see in Bryce Canyon National Park than we could get in just one book. To help plan your stay, stop at the visitor center. You'll be able to find out about rules, pick up permits, and learn how to have a safe trip while you're there.

Mountain lion

Here's a few of the things we missed. Zoom in for a good time!

There are more than 160 kinds of birds in the park, and big animals from coyotes to cougars.

More than 100 million years of history are on display in the rocks of the park! This place has been an ocean, a swamp, a lake, a forest, and a beach.

Animals that have lived here in the past include saber-toothed tigers, dinosaurs, woolly mammoths, and a scary sea creature called a plesiosaur that grew to over 35 feet long!

Cooper's hawk

And, for young adventurers who never quit learning, a whole lot more!

Badger

Z is for **Zooming in**
On everything we've missed.
The things to see and do in Bryce
Make far too long a list!

Z

What do you mean by . . . ?

amphitheater (am´fə thē´ə tər)—a flat or gently sloping area with steep sides

artifacts (är´tə fakt´)—things made by humans; scientists study the tools, pottery, and other artifacts left by ancient people to learn more about them

differential erosion (dif´ə ren´shəl´ i rō´shən)—a process where softer rocks wear away faster than harder rocks, creating the cool shapes you see in Bryce Canyon

erosion (i rō´shən)—wearing away of our planet's surface by water, glaciers, freezing and thawing, and wind

Basket Maker (bas´kit´ ma´kər)—the people who lived in the valleys below the park from about A.D. 1 to A.D. 700; they were named for the intricate baskets they made

cap rock (kap´ rok)—the top layer in a rock formation; when a cap rock is harder than the rocks below it, erosion can create hoodoos

Desert Archaic (dez´ərt´ är kā´ik)—the people who hunted and gathered plants in this region from about 6000 B.C. to A.D. 500; we know about them from stone tools they left

Grand Staircase (grand´ stâr´kas)—a series of cliffs and *plateaus* that drop from the Pink Cliffs of Bryce Canyon National Park all the way toward the rim of the Grand Canyon

hoodoo (hōō´dōō)—a pinnacle, spire, tower or other odd-shaped rock left standing by the forces of erosion.

Mormon (môr´mən)—member of the Church of Jesus Christ of the Latter-Day Saints; Mormons settled hundreds of towns in Utah after fleeing religious persecution in the East in the mid-1800s

Paiute (pī o͞ot´)—the Southern Paiute band of Indians hunted, farmed, and gathered plants in this region from about A.D. 1000 to the late 1800s

plateau (pla tō´)—a flat-topped mountain

Pueblo people (pweb´lō´ pē´pəl)—skilled farmers who grew corn, squash, and beans in this area from about A.D. 700 to A.D. 1250; they built big stone buildings that could shelter many people

Leave No Trace©!

Leave No Trace! is just another way to say . . . leave the park the same or better than you found it. Pack out your trash, and pick up somebody else's, too! Leave all rocks, flowers, *artifacts*, antlers, and bones in their place exactly as you found them. Then others can enjoy the beauty of Bryce Canyon National Park just like you.

More books you'll enjoy!

For Kids

The Bryce Canyon Auto and Hiking Guide, by TULLY STROUD. Bryce Canyon Natural History Association.

Bryce Canyon Coloring Book, by DEBORAH KELLEY. Bryce Canyon Natural History Association.

Bryce Canyon Discovery, by BOBBI SALTS, Illustrations by STEVE PARKER. American Educational Press.

A Kid's Guide to Bryce Canyon, by PAT STUTELBERG-KITELSON, Illustrations by BROOKE FEELEY-CONNOR. Bryce Canyon Natural History Association.

Mountain Wildlife, by MARJ DUNMIRE. Pegasus Graphics.

Wild Utah Coloring Book, by HELEN HENKEL LARSON, Illustrations by GARY A. BLOOMFIELD. Earthwalk Press.

Wildlife of Cactus and Canyon Country, by MARJ DUNMIRE. D&L Distribution.

From KC Publications

Bryce Canyon: The Story Behind the Scenery, by JOHN BEZY.

in pictures...Bryce Canyon: The Continuing Story, by SUSAN COLCLAZER.

The Southern Paiutes, by LA VAN MARTINEAU.

What Does the Future Hold?

Though far, far away, Bryce Canyon has been changed by humans. Pioneers cut trees to build homes. They grazed sheep and cattle.

Human activities were limited when Bryce Canyon became a national forest in the early 1900s. In 1928 it was protected even more, as a national park.

Now Bryce Canyon draws so many visitors that this red-rock fairyland has become crowded. A shuttle system was developed to reduce traffic and keep the magic in the park.

The future of Bryce is bright when everyone does their part. So park your car and ride the shuttle! Stay on trails, pack out trash, and learn all you can about the natural world and things that threaten it.

Bryce Canyon is for all the world's people. Every visitor plays a part in its future. You, too, can make a difference!

For more information about Bryce Canyon National Park, visit **www.nps.gov/brca**

KC Publications has been the leading publisher of colorful, interpretive books about National Park areas, public lands, Indian lands, and related subjects for over 37 years. We have 6 active series—over 125 titles—with Translation Packages in up to 8 languages for over half the areas we cover. Write, call, or visit our web site for our full-color catalog.

Our series are:

The Story Behind the Scenery® – Compelling stories of over 65 National Park areas and similar Public Land areas. Some with Translation Packages.

in pictures... The Continuing Story® – A companion, pictorially oriented, series on America's National Parks. All titles have Translation Packages.

For Young Adventurers™ – Dedicated to young seekers and keepers of all things wild and sacred. Explore America's Heritage from A to Z.

Voyage of Discovery™ – Exploration of the expansion of the western United States.

Indian Culture and the Southwest – All about Native Americans, past and present.

Calendars – For National Parks and Southwest Indian culture, in dramatic full color, and a companion Color Your Own series, with crayons.

To receive our full-color catalog featuring over 125 titles—Books, Calendars, Screen Scenes, Videos, Audio Tapes, and other related specialty products:

Call (800-626-9673), fax (702-433-3420), write to the address below, Or visit our web site at www.kcpublications.com

Published by KC Publications, 3245 E. Patrick Ln., Suite A, Las Vegas, NV 89120.

Inside back cover:
Taking a break beneath a bristlecone pine.

Back cover:
Deer fawn with butterfly.

Created, Designed, and Published in the U.S.A.
Printed by Tien Wah Press (Pte.) Ltd, Singapore
Color Separations by United Graphic Pte. Ltd